34028051753276

D1443755

Historical Atlases of South Asia,
Central Asia, and the Middle East™

A HISTORICAL ATLAS OF

OMAN

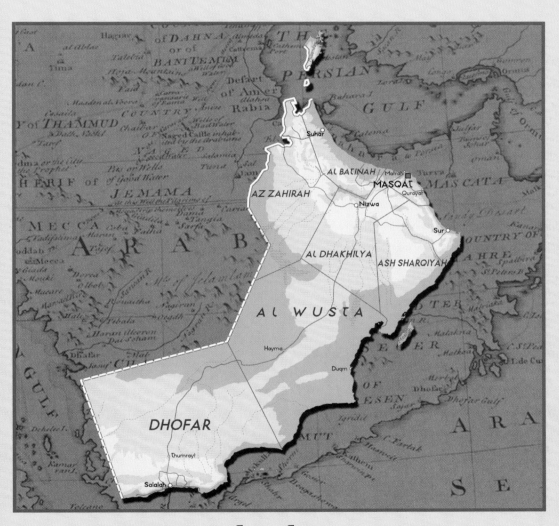

Michael Isaac

The Rosen Publishing Group, Inc., New York

For Sherri

Published in 2004 by The Rosen Publishing Group, Inc.
29 East 21st Street, New York, NY 10010

Library of Congress Cataloging-in-Publication Data

Isaac, Michael
A historical atlas of Oman/ by Michael Isaac. — 1st ed.
p. cm. — (Historical atlases of South Asia, Central Asia, and the Middle East)
Summary: Maps and text chronicle the history of the Sultanate of Oman, located on the southeastern Arabian Peninsula.
Includes bibliographical references and index.
Contents: Early Oman — Arab dominance — Invasions and independence — The Sa'id dynasty — Rebellions — Qabus ibn Sa'id — Modern Oman.
ISBN 0-8239-4500-6
1. Oman — History — Maps for children. 2. Oman — Maps for children. [1. Oman — History. 2. Atlases.] I. Title. II. Series.

G2249.71.S1I8 2004
911'.5353 — dc22

2003055016

Manufactured in the United States of America

Cover images: The seventeenth-century blue-domed mosque in Nizwa, Oman; traditional Omani daggers known as khanjars; and the current sultan and prime minister of Oman, Qabus ibn Sa'id are shown here along with an eighteenth-century map of Asia by Emanuel Bowen that features the Arabian Peninsula (background) and a contemporary map of Oman.

Contents

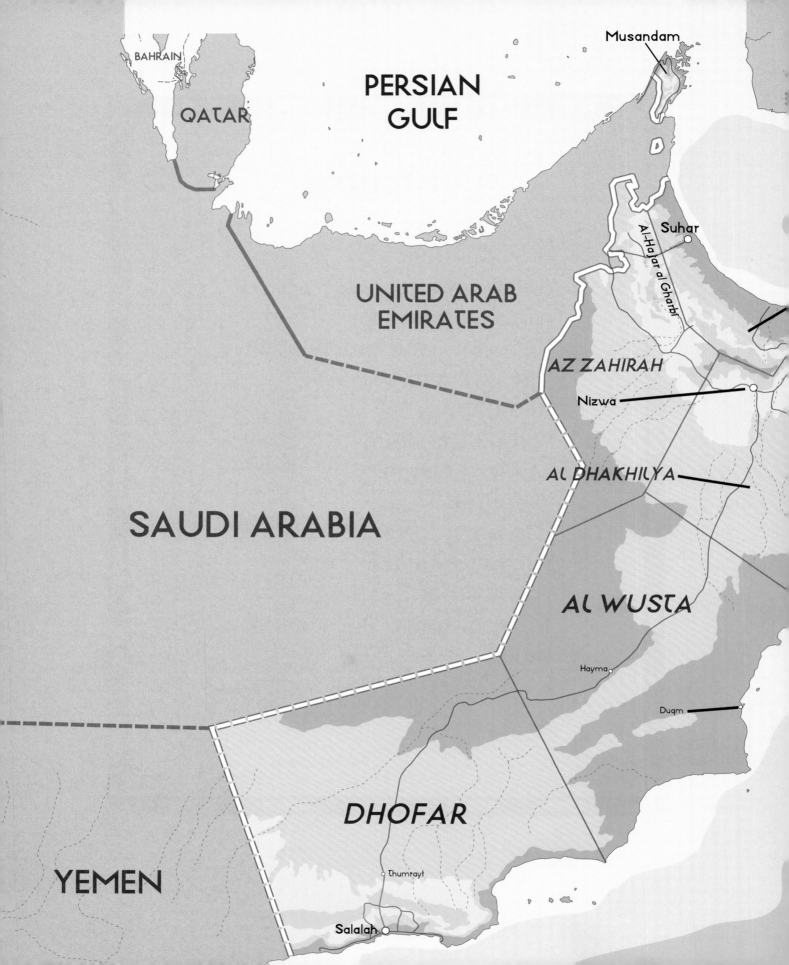

IRAN

AL BATINAH

Gulf of
Oman

Matrah

MASQAT

Qurayat

Sur

ASH SHARQIYAH

Masirah

ARABIAN SEA

INTRODUCTION

The Sultanate of Oman is a country situated along the southeastern Arabian Peninsula. Oman is bordered by Yemen and Saudi Arabia on its western boundaries and in the north by the United Arab Emirates. The country's extensive coastline, which runs along the Arabian Sea and the Gulf of Oman, offers its citizens picturesque beauty, a growing tourist industry, and the ability to easily export oil (first discovered there in 1964) around the world. The country's other main sources of income lie in its hearty natural gas resources, copper mines, and fishing industry. Oman is divided into six regions, and its capital city is Masqat.

The land now known as Oman has a long and fascinating history that dates back to the Stone Age. Portugal conquered Oman from 1508 to 1659, when the Ottoman Empire replaced it as a leading regional force. The Turks ruled Oman until 1741. At that

This contemporary map of Oman shows its geographical position along the southeastern Arabian Peninsula, along the Gulf of Oman and the Arabian Sea. Oman is a vast desert plain that is divided into six regions and two governorates: Al Dhakhilya, Ash Sharqiyah, Al Wusta, Al Batinah, Az Zahirah, Masqat, Musandam, and Dhofar. As a desert country nearly without land suitable for agriculture, Oman faces many challenges, including how to properly provide water and food for its growing population. Until 1999, Oman's border with the United Arab Emirates was disputed by both nations. A treaty between them, finalized in 2002, settled the boundary shown on this map.

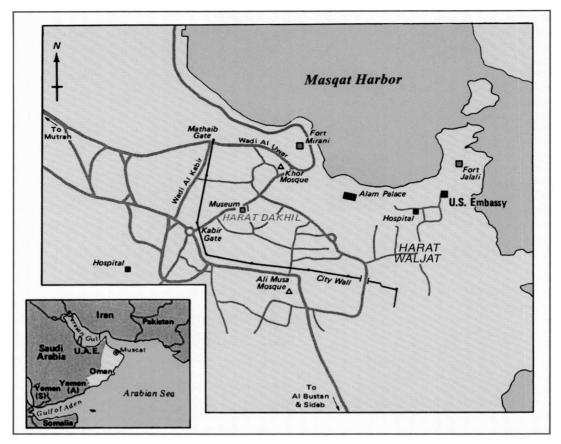

The port of Masqat in Oman, shown on this contemporary map, is strategically situated at the mouth of the Gulf of Oman. As an important trading port since the sixth century BC, Masqat has been the capital of Oman since 1741 and was once a trading center of African slaves. The Portuguese captured Masqat in 1508 and held the city for more than 150 years before Ottoman Turks dominated it.

time, they were forced out by Ahmed ibn Sa'id of Yemen, who started the nation's line of royal leaders. By the early nineteenth century, Oman had formed close ties with Great Britain for military protection. As a result, Great Britain had gained great power, then controlling Zanzibar (a chain of several islands off the coast of East Africa), parts of Iran, and sections of present-day Pakistan.

Today, Oman is an ally of the United States. It has maintained diplomatic relations with other Western nations, too, as well as countries in the Middle East. The country has been a part of the United Nations and the Arab League since 1971. At the time of Iraq's invasion of Kuwait in 1990, Oman offered its support. In an effort to assist the United States–led coalition to free Kuwait, the Omani government allowed U.S. forces to utilize its military bases. Oman's bases were again used in the 2001 United States–led attack against Afghanistan's Taliban government and Osama bin Laden.

1 EARLY OMAN

Oman lies along the coast of the Arabian Peninsula, and its 120,000 square miles (311,000 square kilometers) cover some of the most diverse landscapes in the Gulf States. Oman has 1,300 miles (2,092 km) of coastline that run along the Arabian Sea and the Gulf of Oman. The mountainous northern tip, known as Musandam, slopes steeply into the Strait of Hormuz. Running along the northern Batinah coast is the 400-mile (644-km) Al-Hajar Mountains, which form two distinct ranges. These ranges are called the Al-Hajar al Gharbi Mountains, or Western Al-Hajar, and the Al-Hajar ash Shargi, or Eastern Al-Hajar. The highest peak lies in the western al Gharbi range and is known as Jebal Sham, or "Mountain of the Sun." The coastal side receives more rain than the southern side, which leads to the vast arid desert known as Rub al-Khali, or "Empty Quarter." The southern coast receives seasonal monsoon rains, sometimes as much as 25 inches (64 centimeters) annually, producing its green tropical scenery. The northern side, however, is cut off from the rain, and its vegetation is extremely sparse. Temperatures in Oman can reach 130°F (54°C), making it one of the hottest places in the world.

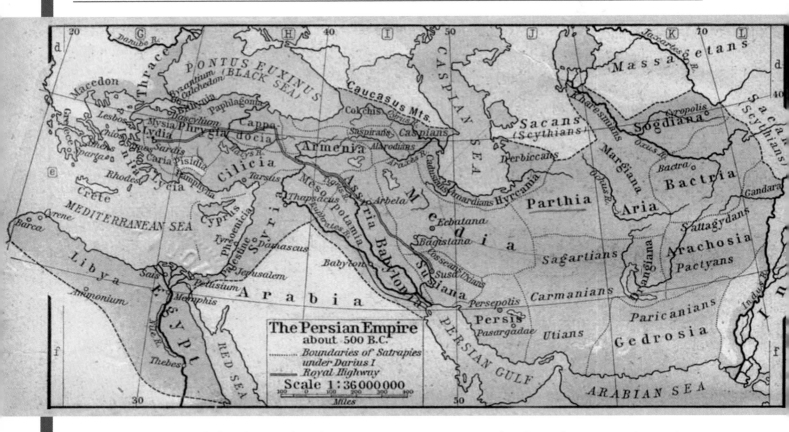

Southern Arabia, including the area later known as Oman, was conquered in the sixth century BC by Persian armies under Cyrus the Great. The Persians were a nomadic Indo-European people who emerged from the Mesopotamian region. The Persian Empire became the first great world empire with territories that stretched from present-day Iran to Greece, Egypt, Israel, parts of India, and throughout the Arabian Peninsula.

Earliest Civilization

Archaeologists studying the history of the Arabian Peninsula have found evidence that people have lived in the lands later known as Oman as early as the third millennium BC. This early civilization survived through the end of the last ice age by hunting animals such as gazelles and wild goats, and by gathering wild fruits and berries. Artifacts recovered from tombs seem to indicate that its people originated in what is now Iraq or southern Iran. Over time, these prehistoric hunter-gatherers began to build more permanent settlements. Archaeologists digging in the Al-Hajar Mountains for instance, as well as in the southern region of Dhofar, have unearthed prehistoric artifacts such as knives and axes made from flint. These simple tools suggest that the people of this period had developed technology advanced enough to grow their own food and raise animals.

Oman is a nation that is bounded by ocean waters and rugged mountains. Much of its population is nomadic, a people referred to as bedouin, who normally travel Oman's desert plains by camel. The arid desert plains of Oman, an ecosystem that has recently been threatened by the country's push toward modernization, are home to more than 130 plant and animal species.

By 3000 BC, Oman was inhabited by a civilization that left behind a wealth of artifacts, revealing much about its culture. The artfully decorated pottery that archaeologists have found in the region appears to have been crafted with a potter's wheel. There is also evidence that the society built dams, used donkeys to transport goods, and built homes out of limestone. Many of the beehive-shaped stone tombs believed by some archaeologists to have held their dead are still standing.

The most important find for archaeologists, however, was an abundance of copper. Early Sumerian records note a society in the region called Magan that mined its extensive copper resources and used the valuable metal in trading. Today, most archaeologists are certain that Magan existed on land that is now a part of Oman. Its people used sophisticated

Bronze Age structures, such as the remains of these beehive tombs, are more than 4,000 years old. Similar tombs are scattered across the Eastern Al-Hajar Mountains, located approximately 62 miles (100 kilometers) southeast of Masqat. Archaeologists remain uncertain about the origin of the tombs or the purpose they may have served.

technology to mine the copper ore from the earth and then extract the metal from the ore. The copper was loaded onto ships and exported to lands that lacked copper deposits, such as Mesopotamia, Elam, and Sumer, where it was then used to craft weapons. The Magan mines traded between 48 and 60 tons (44 and 54 metric tons) of copper per year. In exchange, they received lumber and finished goods. Oman's copper was mined in the inland settlements of Lasail and Arja, and it was shipped from the Batinah coast.

After the copper trade was no longer active, the southernmost region of Dhofar developed into a profitable trading center. Dhofar was one of a few places in the world that grew the trees that produced frankincense, a fragrant gum that was an important part of rituals practiced by various cultures in the Middle East and the Mediterranean region. It could be burned as incense or used as medicine. Ancient Egypt, Persia, and Rome were some of the powerful societies whose temples imported frankincense. The people of southern Arabia acquired great wealth from the frankincense trade, according to historians such as Pliny the Elder, who wrote about the success of the incense trade in the first century AD. Arabs exported about 3,000 tons each year on what archaeologists call the "incense road," the remains of which are still being sought. Frankincense is still produced in Dhofar today.

The ancient civilizations that lived on the land now known as Oman founded some of the earliest centers of international trade. This was not only a result of the land's valuable resources but also its geography. Located along an important coastline of the Arabian Sea, the

The harbor of Khor Rori leads out to the Arabian Sea and is located in Dhofar, Oman. During ancient times, Khor Rori was the center of frankincense trade and was known as Sumhuram, a city that dates back to the fourth century BC. In the medieval period, Khor Rori was among the first ports that focused on trade to and from India.

region became a stopping point for merchants on their way to and from India and East Africa. As trade developed further, it became clear that the region's leaders would have a powerful influence over Arabian shipping routes. Cities were established along the coast to accommodate commercial travelers. As a result, the coastal areas developed a culture that became increasingly distinct from the interior. International trade made Oman wealthy but also brought about changes that created great conflicts.

Persian Colonization

In 563 BC, Cyrus the Great of Persia sent his army into southern Arabia (Oman) and successfully conquered the north. The city of Suhar became the capital of the Persian Empire. As the Persians acquired land in Arabia, they brought their technology to the region. They introduced a system of irrigation known as *aflaj*, which has

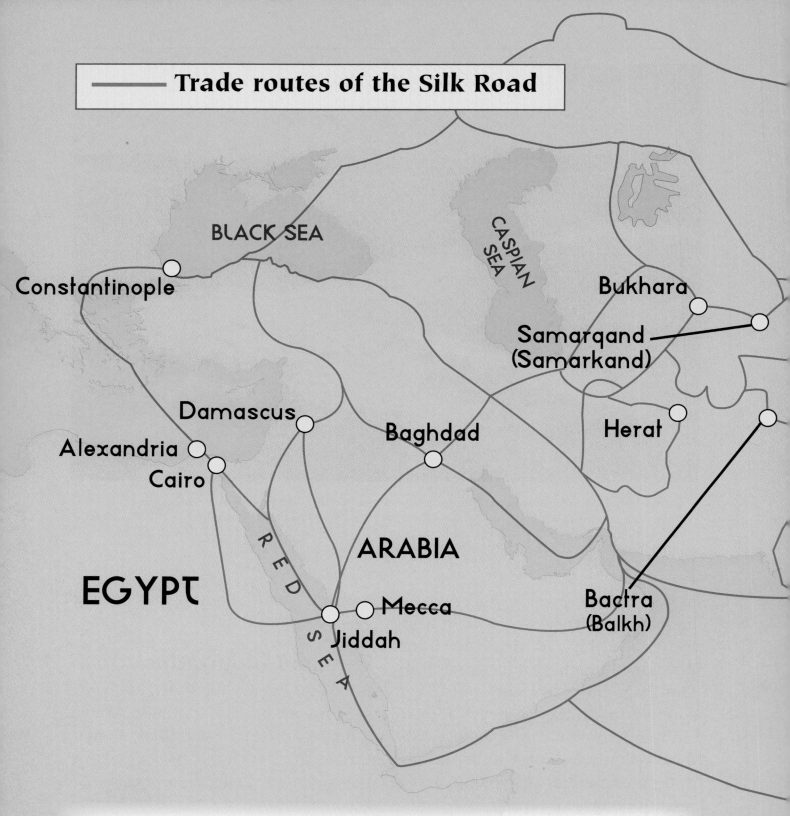

Trade routes of the Silk Road

BLACK SEA

CASPIAN SEA

Constantinople

Bukhara

Samarqand (Samarkand)

Damascus

Baghdad

Herat

Alexandria

Cairo

RED SEA

ARABIA

EGYPT

Mecca

Jiddah

Bactra (Balkh)

The Silk Road, a system of ancient trade routes over land and sea, provided an exchange of goods from China to the Mediterranean world via Mesopotamia, Persia (Iran), and Central Asia. Through the exchange of goods, technologies, and ideas, the development of world civilizations was profoundly affected. These trade routes experienced several periods of heavy use between 150 BC and AD 1300.

Frankincense

The earliest recorded use of frankincense can be traced back to the Egyptian queen Hatshepsut, who ground the charred remains of the resin into eyeliner called kohl. Frankincense is more often remembered as one of the gifts given by the magi (wise men) to the infant Jesus. It is for this reason that frankincense is commonly burnt by Christians during Christmas.

Found mainly in southern Arabia and in Africa, frankincense is harvested from trees of the genus *Boswellia* by making deep incisions into its trunk. After months of exposure to air, a milky resin called oleo hardens to produce the yellowish "tears" that are commonly burned as incense.

Frankincense has been used in religious rituals and for medicinal purposes for thousands of years. The Arab physician Ibn Sina, known in the West as Avicenna (AD 980–1037), believed that frankincense was excellent for a variety of ailments, such as tumors, vomiting, dysentery, and fevers. Today, Oman continues to produce some of the rarest and most fragrant frankincense in the world, though foreign trade of the resin has largely decreased in contemporary culture.

Although frankincense is no longer the chief export of Oman, it is still burned throughout the country and the entire Arabian Peninsula. Today, frankincense is seldom used for medicinal purposes, although ancient texts refer to the resin as an antidote for ailments including hemlock poisoning, bronchial congestion, and nausea. The Romans used frankincense for both ceremonial purposes and private use. Frankincense is now used primarily for religious rituals. The natural golden resin or man-made incense is burned at various times by Jews, Christians, Hindus, and Muslims.

been vital to agriculture throughout Oman's history. In this system, a vertical shaft is used to reach the water held in porous rocks that lie underground. A tunnel runs up from the bottom of the shaft to the surface or to an underground pool where it can be collected with a bucket. Since each *falaj* (a single channel) may be several miles long, this system of irrigation required a significant amount of labor and maintenance.

The conquest of Arabia gave Persia control of the shipping routes

The ancient aflaj irrigation system captures mountain water and controls its movement in man-made underground channels. The system uses gravity to lead the water down the mountains to the desert plains. Each single channel is known as a falaj. The history of the aflaj irrigation system in desert countries dates back to the Persian era when settlers introduced the qanat system in Persepolis around 500 BC.

in the Persian Gulf and Arabian Sea. Merchants from distant lands continued to pass through Arabia's ports. As a result, people living in coastal cities were exposed to many cultures and religions, including Judaism, Christianity, and Zoroastrianism, the religion begun by the Persians. Islam, however, which had emerged by AD 700, was the religion that would have the greatest influence of all in Arabia.

2 ARAB DOMINANCE

While the Persians were controlling the population of people living in Arabia, their population was undergoing a drastic change. From approximately AD 100, tribes from southern Arabia were migrating into the Jalan region of Oman. The changing population, along with the introduction of Islam, would soon mean the end of Persian rule.

In ancient times, various tribes, such as the Semitic groups Baida and Ariba, journeyed to Oman, but over time these tribes became extinct. By the second century AD, the two most prominent Arab tribes that were migrating into Oman were the Qahtan and the Nizar. The Qahtan came from southwestern Arabia, and the Nizar were from northwestern Arabia. These groups were bitter rivals. People also migrated into Oman from Mar'ib (in present-day Yemen)

Alexandria

EGYPT

This map illustrates the spread of Islam throughout the Arabian Peninsula and the surrounding empires. Arabs living in southern Arabia figure prominently among Islam's earliest converts. According to historians, Muhammad sent military leaders to convert Arabs, some of whom were Christian, and Persians living in Arabia who practiced Zoroastrianism. Muhammad recognized Christians and Jews as "people of the book," whose scriptures he considered God's word much like his own revelations. Arab Muslims referred to Christians and Jews as *dhimmis* (tolerated subjects) and allowed them to practice Christianity and Judaism if they refrained from converting Muslims, lived under Muslim authority, and paid additional taxes.

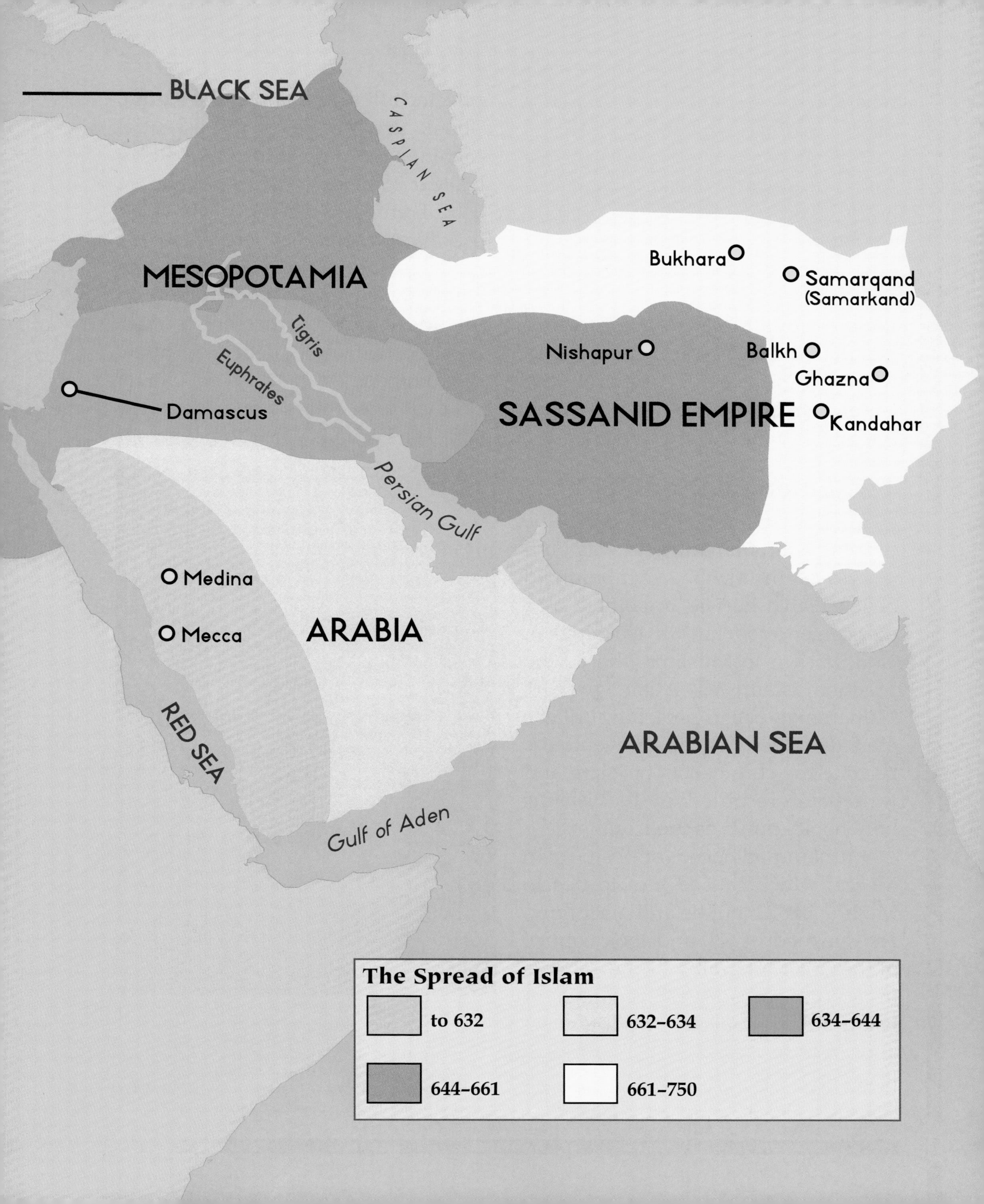

BLACK SEA

CASPIAN SEA

MESOPOTAMIA

Tigris

Euphrates

Damascus

Persian Gulf

Bukhara

Samarqand
(Samarkand)

Nishapur

Balkh

Ghazna

Kandahar

SASSANID EMPIRE

O Medina

O Mecca

ARABIA

ARABIAN SEA

RED SEA

Gulf of Aden

The Spread of Islam

	to 632		632–634		634–644
	644–661		661–750		

when a great dam collapsed and destroyed their irrigation system.

The Arab population acquired a solid footing in central Oman, eventually making its way to the Persian-controlled lands in the north. At first, these quarreling Arab groups rejected Persian rule, but they were not a serious threat to the Persians. During the seventh century AD, when Arabs became united under Islam, Persian control of Suhar and the Batinah coast were threatened.

The Emergence of Islam

Islam is a religion founded by the prophet Muhammad, who was born in Mecca in AD 570. Muhammad believed that he was appointed as a messenger to spread the teachings of God, known to Muslims (those who practice Islam) as Allah. In 610, Muhammad began preaching Allah's message. These teachings eventually became the core beliefs of Islam and were later recorded in the Islamic holy book known as the Koran.

Muhammad faced opposition in Mecca, which caused him to flee to Medina in 622, but he and his followers returned in 630 and took control of the city. Muhammad's messengers in Mecca spread the teachings of Islam throughout the Middle East and North Africa. Muhammad's teachings were written down and collected after his death in the Koran, a book that preserves the essential teachings of Islam. Muslims believe this text is the exact word of Allah.

Muhammad's messengers traveled to Suhar, where they promoted his teachings and gained many converts among the city's Arab population. In 630, Muhammad's messenger Amr Ibn al-As delivered a letter to leaders of prominent Arab tribes in Oman, and they soon embraced the new religion. The Persians who did not accept

Pilgrims depicted in this fifteenth-century manuscript arrive in Mecca after their journey known as the *hajj*, one of the five pillars of Islam. The other four include believing in Allah with Muhammad as his prophet, praying facing Mecca five times a day, giving alms (charity) to the poor, and fasting during Ramadan.

Islam were soon expelled. It was during this period that Suhar was ruled by the Umayyad dynasty, the first powerful Muslim dynasty, which lasted from AD 640 to 750. The Umayyad seat of power was in Damascus, a city that entered a golden age as the center of Islam. With Islam now the official religion in Oman, Arab migration increased and Arabic became the dominant language. To this day, Omanis are proud that their ancestors were among the first converts to Islam, accepting the reli-

The blue-domed mosque in Nizwa, located near Fort Nizwa, was built in the mid-seventeenth century by Iman Sultan bin Saif, the first imam of the Al-Ya'ribi dynasty.

gion in the seventh century during the Prophet's lifetime.

The Ibadite Imamate

During the seventh century, Omanis converted to Ibadite Islam, which is a division, of the religion that they have maintained throughout their history. Ibadite Islam originated in Iraq but was unable to survive throughout all of Oman because the region's most powerful spiritual leader, or caliph, suppressed competing forms of Islam. Today, Oman's continued practice of Ibadite Islam, which is practiced by about 75 percent of the nation's Muslim population, has made it unique among Islamic nations. Ibadite mosques have fewer decorations and tend to be simpler than those built by other branches of Islam. Ibadite prayer ceremonies do not use music.

One of the sect's core beliefs is its opposition to Muslim congregations being led by hereditary rulers, such as the caliph in Baghdad. Instead, a council of religious scholars elects a leader, known as an *imam*. Each elected imam in Oman is expected to help his nation become the perfect Islamic nation by leading his followers both spiritually and militarily. The first Omani imam, Julanda bin Mas'ud, was elected in 751. The election of a single imam helped unite the various tribal groups in Oman.

In 746, the Omani Ibadites, then led by Talib al-Haqq, rebelled against the Umayyad rulers and drove them from Oman. Strengthened by their successful revolt, the Ibadites expanded their conquest through the Arabian Peninsula. By 748, they had conquered Medina, one of the holiest cities in the Islamic world, but their victory was fleeting. The Umayyad Empire reclaimed Medina, but their empire soon declined. The 'Abbasids,

Fort Nizwa was strategically erected at the crossroads of caravan routes in order to protect Arabs who were traveling with valuable goods. Built under Imam Sultan bin Saif during the seventeenth century, the fort has sturdy walls able to resist repeated mortar fire. Its features include a central tower, turrets, secret shafts, false doors, and wells.

whose leader was the caliph in Baghdad, dominated the Umayyad Empire over a ten-year period beginning in 740. The caliph intended to bring the entire Muslim world under his rule, but he was unable to subdue the Ibadites. Julanda bin Mas'ud was killed in battle with the 'Abbasids in 752, and it was not until 801 that his successor, Warith bin Kaab, was elected.

The imam had more followers in central Oman than on its coast. This is probably because the coast was constantly exposed to foreign travelers and cultures, while its interior was isolated. People living in the interior felt a greater loyalty to their communities. The two regions competed to be the center of power in Oman. The inland city of Nizwa was Oman's most powerful urban center during the ninth century. This changed within a century, when the coast became more powerful. International trade brought prosperity to communities along the coast, with the city of Suhar becoming the strongest and wealthiest of all. This ended in 971 when the Persians attacked Oman, demolishing Suhar. For the next several centuries, the country's most powerful city was Qalhat.

While the Persians' control spread along the coast of Oman, imams continuously held the interior. In 1154,

Bahla Fort

One of Oman's most famous sites is the Bahla Fort, located in the oasis of Bahla about 16 miles (25 km) west of Nizwa. The fort is believed to have been constructed first by the Persians before the emergence of Islam, and then renovated several more times, first in AD 830, then in 1624, and finally in 1868. Originally constructed from mud brick and stone, the fort once contained some fifteen entrances along its wall and as many as 132 towers. Later materials included clay, straw, brick, wood, and plaster. In 1988, the Bahla Fort site was added to the World Heritage List of endangered sites, recognized by the United Nations Educational, Scientific, and Cultural Organization (UNESCO), and is considered a monument of global importance.

The Bahla Fort is located in Bahla, Oman, an early medieval capital and an oasis named after the Banu Nebhan tribe, which governed the region from the twelfth to the fifteenth century. Other archaeological evidence suggests that Bahla might also have been an important site in the ancient world. Prominent features of the Bahla Fort are its many towers, including its "Tower of Wind," known as Burj-al-Reh. Conservation efforts are now being undertaken to reduce the deterioration of the fort, which tends to crumble more and more each year with the passing of Oman's rainy season.

Sultan Khalifa II, pictured on this postage stamp, enjoyed a long and peaceful reign of Zanzibar from 1911 until 1960. Zanzibar was controlled by Oman until 1856 and was a British protectorate from 1890. Zanzibar prospered as a peaceful island chain and escaped direct involvement in both world wars. It is now part of the United Republic of Tanzania.

the imams' power was challenged by a dynasty of kings who ruled from the island of Hormuz. For the next two centuries, no imams were elected. The coast of Oman was attacked during this period by empires based in present-day Iran, Iraq, and Turkey that sought control of the region's lucrative trade routes. At the same time, Oman extended its control along the coast of East Africa. Omanis invaded and struggled to keep control of the islands of Pemba and Zanzibar, as well as the African port towns of Dar es Salaam, Lamu, Malindi, and Mombasa.

3 INVASIONS AND INDEPENDENCE

Until the fifteenth century, Oman had no contact with Europeans. This changed in 1488, which became a turning point in the nation's history. It was this year that Portuguese explorer Vasco da Gama navigated around Africa's Cape of Good Hope, bringing him in contact with Omani-controlled lands along the East African coast. Arab navigators that he met in Malindi (in present-day Kenya) showed da Gama the shipping routes that led from their ports to India. Tragically, the people living along the East African coast were repaid with brutal violence as the Portuguese proceeded to colonize the region and take control of the profitable trade business.

Portuguese Colonization

During this era, the Portuguese surpassed many other nations with their mastery of sea travel and sea combat. They built thick-hulled ships that could withstand long voyages, permitting Portuguese explorers to land on distant shores. The Portuguese fleets were also equipped with heavy cannons that were powerful enough to blast through the hulls of their competitors' ships. Arab *dhows* (boats) lacked the strength and the weaponry needed to withstand the force of the Portuguese invaders.

Lisbon

SANTIAGO

MAR

ATLANTIC

LINEA EQUINOCIAL

AFRICA

BRASIL

STA HELE

The sea routes of Vasco da Gama (1460–1524) are shown on this map. Da Gama made progress down the western coast of Africa in search of a sea route to India following the paths of earlier navigators who had traveled as far south as Africa's Cape of Good Hope. Da Gama continued sailing into unknown territory along the eastern coast of Africa while he dodged Arab strongholds. By 1498, da Gama had found a passage to India, securing valuable trade routes for Portugal. Portugal controlled coastal Oman from about 1508 to 1659.

Cape of Good Hope

In 1506, five Portuguese ships led by Alfonso de Albuquerque made their way to the coast of Oman. By the following year, Masqat and other coastal settlements had fallen to Portuguese rule. The major purpose of the invasion was to secure Portuguese control of the trade routes to the territories that Portugal ruled in India, such as Calicut. The Portuguese realized that colonizing the island of Hormuz was the key to preserving their control of the region's waterways. When their fleet attacked Hormuz, it was controlled by Abbas I, the shah of Persia (Iran). Persia's army lacked the strength to fight off the invasion, and Hormuz became Portugal's main base in Oman. Portugal left Hormuz's Persian leaders in power and profited from the fees that they were forced to pay.

Portugal controlled Oman's coast for 143 years, but other than its forts in Masqat, very few signs of its presence remain. This seems to indicate that Portugal was more concerned

These Arab vessels docked at the port of Sur in eastern Oman are known as *dhows*. Dhows have been a fixture in Persian Gulf waters for centuries and are commonly used for fishing expeditions, traveling, pearl diving, and recreation. Dhows actually refer to a variety of Arab boats, though most are made of wood and have similar distinctions, including a high stern and a low bow that sweeps upward.

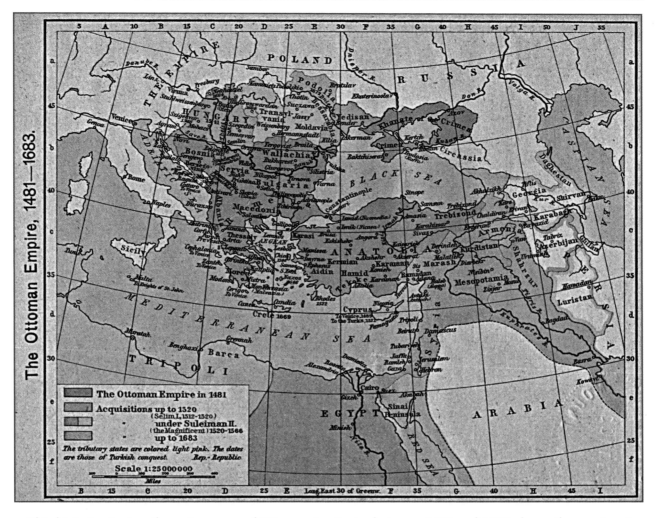

The Ottoman Empire, 1481–1683.

This historic nineteenth-century map of Ottoman territories between 1481 and 1683 shows the empire at various stages of development. The Ottoman Empire reached its golden age under the Sultan Suleiman II, who reigned between 1520 and 1566. Ottoman military strength and territorial gains had increased steadily since 1326, but the greatest expansion occurred during the sixteenth century, when the Ottomans took control of parts of Arabia.

with protecting its trade routes to India than developing the land in Oman. Portugal's hold on the region would eventually slip, beginning in the 1500s when the Ottoman Turks captured Masqat. The Turks took control of Egypt in 1517 and continued their invasions along the Arabian coast. They attacked Masqat several times but were unable to take control from the Portuguese for long.

The Ya'rubid Dynasty

Nasir bin Muhammad, the "sun of salvation," was elected imam in 1624. Although Ibadite Islam was founded on the belief that imams should be elected, Nasir bin Muhammad was succeeded by a dynasty of imams who were born into the Yarub clan. In the seventeenth century, this line of imams, known as the Ya'rubid dynasty, became powerful enough to drive the Portuguese out of Oman.

Unable to remove the Portuguese on their own, leaders in the region sought the help of other Western countries. Abbas I was eager to take back control of Hormuz. He asked both the British and the Dutch for help, but it was the British government that led the fight to recapture the island in 1622. In return, the British received half of the revenues from the Iranian ports.

The British became instrumental in defeating the Portuguese throughout Oman. In 1646, Imam Nasir bin Muhammad signed a treaty with the British East India Company, which marked the beginning of a long rela- tionship between Great Britain and Oman. The British company received trading rights in Oman, and its mer- chants were permitted to practice their religion. British citizens and company employees were also sub- jected to a separate judicial system. Bin Muhammad is credited with lead- ing the fight that ended Portugal's control of Suhar, but by the time of his death in 1647, the Portuguese still controlled the remaining coast. Bin Muhammad's cousin Sultan bin Saif finally defeated Portugal in 1649, end- ing Portuguese colonization in Oman. Many people in present-day Oman consider this year the time of their nation's independence.

With the Portuguese weakening and dispersed, imams ruled from Masqat, uniting the coast and interior under one leader for the first time in

Abbas I, also known as Abbas the Great (1587–1629), the Safavid shah of Persia, is shown in this sixteenth-century fresco charging an Uzbek warrior. Abbas is remembered for saving the Safavid Empire from extinction against Ottoman and Uzbek forces. He also led the empire through a tremendous period of cultural growth and territorial reconquest. Under Abbas's lead- ership, the once diminished empire regained the cities Herat, Tabriz, and Baghdad, achieving again the territorial expanse of the grander borders it had seen under Ismail I, who reigned over the empire from 1501 to 1526.

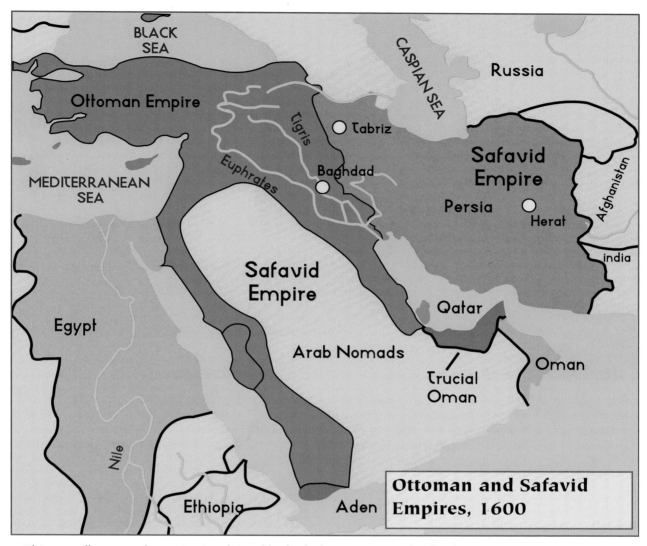

Ottoman and Safavid Empires, 1600

This map illustrates the territories claimed by both the Ottoman and Safavid Empires in 1600. At the time, both empires were the primary rulers of the Arab and Mediterranean regions. Osman founded the Ottoman Empire in the 1300s in the area that is now present-day Turkey. Between 1516 and 1517, Ottoman forces conquered Arab provinces, while the Safavid Empire, based in Persia (present-day Iran), lasted from 1501 to 1722. Both empires experienced periods of expansion and decline and swapped control of cities such as Tabriz and Baghdad.

1,000 years. During this period of political instability, leadership of Oman often shifted from elected imams to hereditary sultans. The Ya'rubid dynasty expanded and took control of Oman's former African ports from Portugal. At the time, the center of Portuguese trade on the African coast was Fort Jesus in Mombasa. Portugal controlled the fort until 1698, when Oman was able to defeat the Portuguese fleet. With the end of Portuguese rule, Oman's military continued its conquest and

Fort Jesus is located in Kenya, Africa, on a coral ridge overlooking the entrance to the Old Port of Mombasa. The Portuguese built the fort between 1593 and 1598 in order to protect their trade route to India and their African colonies. Fort Jesus is considered one of the best examples of Portuguese military architecture. At various times throughout history, it has changed hands and purposes. Although Fort Jesus is now a historical museum, it was once used as a prison.

captured ports along the Persian Gulf and in Africa and India. Once again, Oman was the center of a wealthy and powerful trading industry.

Civil War

With the Ya'rubid dynasty at an end, various groups competed for power, and Oman's cultural divisions began to reappear. In 1719, Saif ibn Sultan II became the hereditary leader of Oman, leading to a rivalry between warring tribes. The land became divided into two warring regions, each ruled separately by the Hinawai tribe and Ghafiri tribe. This conflict can be traced back to the period when Arab tribes migrated into Oman. Hinawai was populated by descendants of the Qahtan tribe, while Ghafiri had an allegiance to Nizar. No longer able to agree on a ruler, the people of Oman began a violent civil war.

The unrest and chaos in Oman made it vulnerable to another invasion. The Ya'rubid family asked the Persian army to help its side win the civil war. The Persians intervened as requested but instead

This historic map of Turkey, Persia (present-day Iran), and the Arabian Peninsula was created during the eighteenth century by the British cartographer Emanuel Bowen. Although Bowen was a well-known engraver and royal cartographer to both King George II of Britain and King Louis XV of France, he died impoverished and nearly blind for his efforts. This map was originally printed in *The Complete Atlas*.

chose to keep the land that they won for themselves. In 1743, the Persian leader Nadir Shah launched an attack on the coast of Oman, capturing the cities of Matrah and Masqat. The Persians extended their rule along the Batinah coast but were unable to take control of Suhar, a city that was successfully defended by its governor, Ahmad ibn Sa'id. Sa'id was eventually able to turn the tide against the Persians and drive them out of the territory, making him a popular hero. His leadership was powerful enough to unite Oman and bring an end to its civil war. Ahmad ibn Sa'id Al Sa'id became imam of Oman and Zanzibar in 1744, founding the Al Sa'id dynasty.

4 THE AL SA'ID DYNASTY

During his lifetime, Ahmad ibn Sa'id Al Sa'id, originally of Yemen, remained popular throughout Oman. His rule led to permanent changes in the way that Oman's territory would be governed. The dynasty that he began has remained in power to the present day.

Oman's religious leaders were so impressed with Al Sa'id that they elected him imam in 1744. A powerful warrior, he led a navy that was strong enough to fend off the Persian invasion and defeat attacks by pirates. The Persian military was finally forced out of Oman in 1748. As a result of the Omani navy's reputation, the pasha of Barasa, who led the Ottoman Empire, asked the fleet for help with his own battles with Persian invaders. Oman succeeded again against the Persians and formed an important alliance with the Ottoman Empire.

The cartographer Phillip De Bay created this eighteenth-century map of Arabia. The eighteenth century marked a period of civil unrest in Oman. Many factors influenced this chaos. Growing encroachments by the Portuguese and the British to secure trade routes from Arabia to India played a significant role in Oman's instability, while the competing struggle between religious imams and the hereditary line of sultans added to this turmoil. The strife between tribes also competing for power and territory created additional disorder in the region.

A AMSTERDAM,
chez IAN RL ELWE.
MDCCXCII

Lieues Marines de 20 par degré
Lieues Communes de France de 25 par degré

I. DE CHYPE

SYRIE

ASIE

LAURESTAN

KIRAC

CHUSISTAN

PERSE

ARABIE DESERTE

Desert de l'Irac

Desert sans eau
ny habitation

GOLFE PERSIQUE

OMAN

ROYAUME
DE MASCATE

ETAT DU CHERIF DE LA MEQUE

Tropique du Cancer

ARABIE

Pays de Mahre
la plus part sterile et desert

MEDINE

EGYPTE

MER ROUGE

ARABIE PETREE
dependante de l'Egypte

TERRE SAINTE

Bouche du Nil

ROYAUME DE LYEMEN OU DE
L'ARABIE HEUREUSE

Pays de
Seger ou
Schajer

Pays de
Hadramut

ROYAUME
DE CARESEN

Golfe de Taphar

Cap Partaque

LES BUGIENS

Deserts
de Nubie

PAYS DE NUBIE

ROYAUME DE SENNAR
OU
DE NUBIE

ISLE DE SOCOTOR
dependante du Roy de Cara

ROYAUME DES CHANGALA
ou Ethiopiens

ROY AGAUS

R. DAMBEA

ROY DE TIGRE

ROY DE BAGEMDER

DOBAS

DANCALI

ROYAUME D'ETHIOPIE

ABISSINIE

ROYAU
DE
DAWARO

ROYAUME
D'ADEL

MER
DES
INDES

ROYAUME DES GALLES
autrefois soumis au Roi d'Ethiopie

GALLES
ORIENTAUX

ou de ZEILA

LA COTE DESERTE
ou AJAN

ETAT
DU ROY
DE GINGIRO

ROYAUME
DE NAREA

GALLA

ROYAUME
D'ALABA

NATIONS DE GALLES
ou LUBA

ROYAUME
DES Machidas

ROYAUME
DE
MAGADOXO

Oman's military power expanded its influence through the region now known as the United Arab Emirates. Oman was also able to capture Dhofar, which today remains within the nation's borders. Al Sa'id also strengthened Oman's control of its shipping ports along the coast of East Africa.

Ahmad ibn Sa'id Al Sa'id died in 1783, and his son, Sultan ibn Ahmad Al Sa'id, succeeded him as imam in 1806. Ahmad's interest was only with his newly appointed religious authority. He appointed his son, Hamad, to be his deputy, or *wadi*. In effect, Hamad became the person who actually controlled Oman. This new leadership was the beginning of a less traditional administration. Until then, the role of imam was the most powerful position in Omani society. Once the imam's power was limited to his religious authority, the head of the government was a separate and more powerful position.

Oman's new administrative rulers began calling themselves *sayyids*. With this change, the sayyids ruled from a new center of power in Masqat on the coast, while the imam remained in the inland city of al-Rustaq. As a result,

both the coast and the interior of Oman had their own type of leader. Not all of the tribal leaders in the inland region accepted the sayyids' authority. The change in Oman's government created more tension between the two sections of Oman.

Upon Hamad's sudden death in 1792, his uncle, Sayyid Sultan bin Ahmed, took control of Oman. He ruled until his death in 1804, when leadership passed to his heir, Sa'id bin Sultan. Also known as Sultan the Great, Sa'id bin Sultan was the first leader of Oman to officially use the title "sultan" in place of "sayyid." The Arabic word "sultan," which means "a man of authority," was his father's name, and he used it as a sign of his authority.

Sa'id bin Sultan ruled Oman when its trade industry was at the height of its power. Oman had extensive ports along the Persian Gulf and East Africa. The sultan built a second capital in Zanzibar, strengthening his power on the African coast. During Sa'id bin Sultan's reign until 1856, Oman's ships traveled to and from increasingly distant cities, including London and New York. Oman became the first Arab country

Asia, as seen in this 1826 historical map drawn by Joseph Perkins, was experiencing a surge of developing empires and changing borders at the beginning of the nineteenth century. The once powerful Ottoman Empire had lost significant territory and power during this period, the British Empire was in control of India, and the Russian Empire was expanding. Meanwhile, rival tribes were competing for control over the interior Arabian Peninsula while the sultans of Oman were expanding their own trading centers on the African Coast.

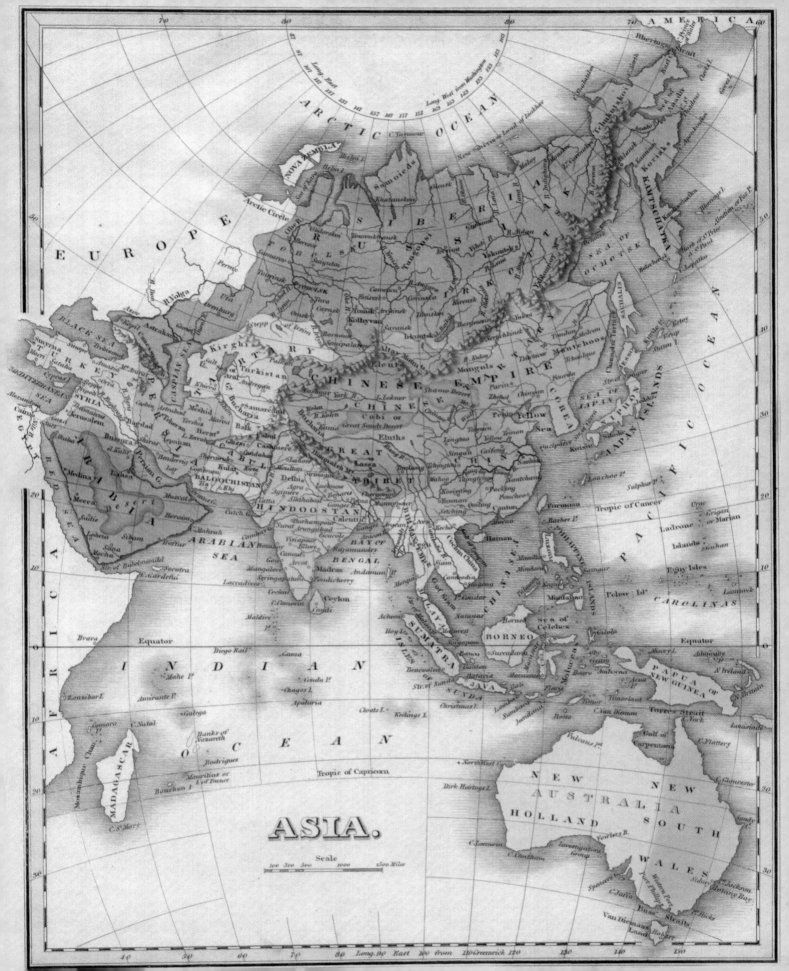

ASIA.

Scale
100 300 500   1000   1500 Miles

to have diplomatic relations with the United States. This early relationship paved the way for the Treaty of Friendship that was signed by the two countries in 1833.

Alliance with England

Although Oman enjoyed great prosperity under Sa'id bin Sultan's rule, this was soon challenged by the followers of Wahhabism, a new form of Islam that was sweeping through the Arabian Peninsula. The Wahhabi movement's founder was Muhammad ibn 'Abd al-Wahhab. He was angered by forms of Islam that worshiped trees, rocks, or tombs of honored men. He believed that these practices violated the Koran's central idea that there is only one god. Muhammad ibn 'Abd al-Wahhab began the Wahhabi movement to return Muslims to what he believed to be true Islam. In 1744, he met with the leader of Ad Dir'iyah, a small town near Riyadh, and the two agreed to begin a mission to create a Wahhabi state. This motivated the Wahhabis to invade Muslim states and spread their religion by force.

When the Wahhabis reached Oman, some of the Ibadite tribes living in the interior region accepted their ideas. Sa'id bin Sultan, however, viewed the Wahhabis as invaders. Although he made every effort to drive them back with his army of 6,500 men, he was unable to defeat them. For assistance, he called on the help of the British. Oman had depended on British support before, but in the past, the Omani leaders dealt only with the British East India Company. By this time, Britain's presence in the Middle East was more extensive than ever before, and its government developed a direct relationship with Oman's leaders.

Sa'id bin Sultan signed a treaty in 1798 that established the British protection of Oman. Britain had as much of an interest in defeating the Wahhabi tribes as the Omanis had, since Wahhabi pirates often damaged the British trading industry by raiding its ships traveling to and from India. The British government did not try to colonize Oman, as it had done with India. Since Great Britain was only concerned with protecting its trade routes to India, it permitted the sultan to continue ruling Oman, but with British protection.

The British government made agreements with the sultan and with tribal leaders living along the coastline. Soon Great Britain signed one truce agreement after another with the tribes who populated Oman's port towns on the Arabian Sea. In doing so, the coast of Oman came to be called Trucial Oman.

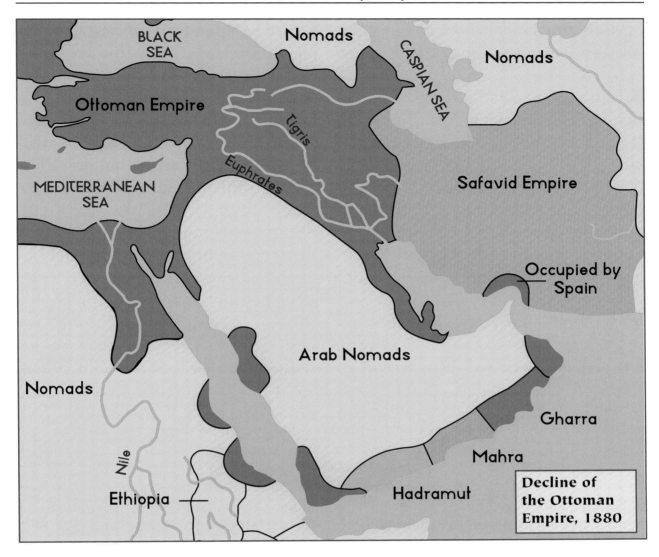

BLACK SEA

Nomads

Nomads

CASPIAN SEA

Ottoman Empire

Tigris

Euphrates

MEDITERRANEAN SEA

Safavid Empire

Occupied by Spain

Arab Nomads

Nomads

Gharra

Mahra

Nile

Hadramut

Ethiopia

Decline of the Ottoman Empire, 1880

The Ottoman Empire began to lose territory beginning in 1798, as shown on this map that shows its holdings in 1880. Territorial losses continued throughout the 1800s and early 1900s, and the once expansive empire crumbled under foreign invaders and lost wars. At the same time, Great Britain, France, and Russia were growing in power and seeking new territories to conquer. British, French, and Russian imperialism began to interfere with Ottoman territories throughout the Middle East.

In 1809, Sa'id bin Sultan launched a joint attack with the British against the Wahhabi tribes. The pirates' base was destroyed, but the Wahhabi attacks did not stop. In 1819, after pirates attacked the sultan's largest ship while he was on board, the Omani and British militaries began another major attack of the Wahhabi pirates. Sa'id bin Sultan needed the help of Britain's military not just to defeat the Wahhabi pirates but also to crush rebellions within Oman's empire. When a revolt broke out in eastern Oman near the port of Sur in 1820, the British and Omani fleets arrived to attack the rebels. Although the first attempt by the British and Omanis to stop the rebellion had ended in defeat, they were successful the following year.

Great Britain's influence in the Middle East continued to increase over the next hundred years. As countries along the Persian Gulf, such as Iraq, Bahrain, and Kuwait,

became dependent on British military protection, they made agreements with Great Britain. These agreements and treaties sometimes interrupted the ability of individual countries to form independent relationships with other nations. The relationship that Oman—as well as many other Gulf States—had with Britain was eventually reduced to a single sweeping treaty. According to the Exclusive Agreement of 1882,

The International Slave Trade

One of the most profitable businesses in Oman's shipping industry was the slave trade. Slave ships made their way from Oman's ports in East Africa to nations around the world where slavery was permitted, including the United States. The British, however, asserted that slavery was immoral. In addition to passing a bill banning slavery in Britain in 1807, the British used their influence to put a stop to slave trading in Oman. Even though many people in Oman made money from slavery, Sa'id bin Sultan agreed in 1822 to forbid the sale of slaves to any Christian nation. The export of slaves was eventually banned completely. The sultan allowed Britain to enforce the rule, permitting its navy to search any ship for illegal slaves.

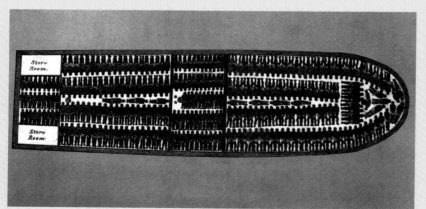

Slave trading became a major enterprise after explorations of the African coast. This lithograph from 1750 illustrates how slaves were crammed into ships headed for the Americas. With people so tightly packed together, it was common for many to become sick. Others died. Slave traders, however, were undeterred by this inhumane treatment and continually earned profits.

none of these states could make an agreement with another country without first obtaining British permission. The purpose of this agreement was to keep Britain's rivals, which included the French and the Dutch, from threatening its trade routes in the Middle East.

Although Oman benefited from Britain's protection, the relationship between the two countries caused a decline in Oman's overall wealth and power. Oman could not compete with European ships that were built with more advanced technology.

Oman also lost money when it was persuaded to abandon its slave trade. Additionally, Great Britain began to dominate trade with India, a business that was once a major source of income for Oman. The poverty that resulted from Oman's declining trade industry caused many Omanis to migrate to Zanzibar. The population of Masqat, once at 55,000, dropped to only 8,000. Through all of these economic setbacks, Sa'id bin Sultan struggled to keep Oman's empire strong. Once he died, however, the turmoil in Oman increased.

5 REBELLIONS

Turkey

Syria ————

Lebanon ————

MEDITERRANEAN
SEA

Palestine ————

Egypt

Nile

RED SEA

Sudan

When Sa'id bin Sultan died in 1856, Oman's empire crumbled. The sultan's two sons fought over who would inherit all of the territories that Oman controlled at the time of their father's death. The British stepped in to settle the dispute by dividing the territories between the two sons. One son, Thuwaini ibn Sa'id al Sa'id, was given control of Zanzibar and the East African colonies. These territories later became an independent state in 1862. The other son, Majid ibn Sa'id al Sa'id, became the ruler of Masqat and Oman. Coastal Masqat was considered a separate territory from the interior of Oman, and Majid ibn Sa'id al Sa'id had authority over both lands. Keeping his control over these territories became his greatest challenge.

British interests in the Persian Gulf revolved around Britain's need to secure its trade routes and possessions in India. Knowing that the sultans of Oman could not control piracy on the Arabian Sea, the British presence in the region increased throughout the nineteenth century. In 1919, the British and French implemented the 1916 Sykes-Picot Agreement, the divisions of which are shown on this map. This agreement divided the Arab world into separate "states" that could be temporarily governed by the British and the French. These borders remained in place until each Arab state became fully independent.

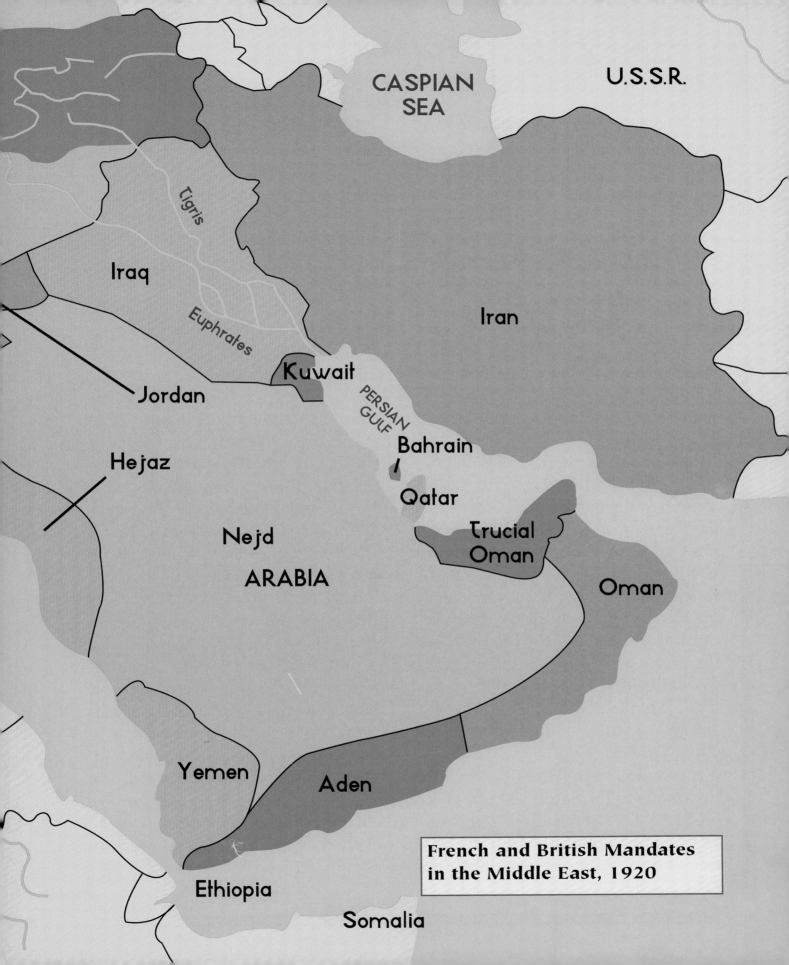

CASPIAN SEA

U.S.S.R.

Tigris

Iraq

Euphrates

Iran

Jordan

Kuwait

PERSIAN GULF

Bahrain

Hejaz

Qatar

Nejd

Trucial Oman

ARABIA

Oman

Yemen

Aden

Ethiopia

Somalia

French and British Mandates in the Middle East, 1920

Ibadite Imamate Rebellion

Many tribes living in the interior had never completely accepted the sultan's rule. Change of power in Oman only increased this tension. Without the profits that once came from Oman's African colonies, the sultan's power was severely weakened. Since the sultan's rule over the tribes was less powerful the farther inland they were based, many people living in the interior began seeking independence. In 1895, tribal rebels from the interior attacked Masqat. Unable to defeat them militarily, the sultan had to pay them to leave.

As they had many times before, the cultural differences between these two distinct parts of Oman created great conflict. In 1868, Azzam ibn Qais al Sa'id declared himself the new imam. In the eyes of the imam's followers, the sultan was not religious enough to lead the country. Omanis wanted a return to the days when one person was both the political and spiritual leader of their country. They also disapproved of the sultan's growing dependence on Great Britain.

Over the next several years, the tribal rebels increased their attacks on Masqat. A new sultan, Turki ibn Sa'id, came to power in 1870. He succeeded in fighting off the rebellions but only with the help of the British military. By this time, British citizens held positions as the sultan's advisers and were in charge of Oman's army. Great Britain recognized that the imam posed a threat to its relationship with the government of Oman, so it supplied the sultan with money and weapons to defeat Azzam ibn Qais al Sa'id. The imam was killed in battle near Matrah in 1871. Turki ibn Sa'id died of a stroke in 1888 and was succeeded by his son, Faysal ibn Turki.

When ibn Turki became sultan, he found himself with little control over the country's interior. Tribal leaders living away from the coast did not accept his authority because they saw him as too dependent on Great Britain. Rebels managed to capture Masqat in 1895, sending the sultan fleeing to safety in Jalal. This time, he felt that the British were making it too difficult for him to recapture Masqat. As a result, ibn Turki resorted to seeking protection from France, Britain's major rival. The British government took immediate steps to prevent France from fulfilling the sultan's request. Great Britain threatened to destroy Masqat if the sultan did not agree to go into exile. Now humiliated, ibn Turki surrendered.

When Taymur ibn Faysal became sultan in 1913, he had no power over

Oman's interior. In the same year, Salim ibn Rashid al Harthi was elected imam. He united the interior tribes and strengthened them to launch a new series of attacks against the sultan. With British support, the sultan defeated each attack, but he could not avoid the rebellion. Great Britain helped to bring a temporary end to the dispute in 1920. At this time, Great Britain brought the two sides together to sign the Treaty of Seeb. With this agreement, the imam was given authority of the interior, while the sultan remained in power of Masqat.

The Discovery of Oil

By the early part of the twentieth century, Oman's days as a powerful center had ended. With its economy in decline, it was not clear if Oman would continue to prosper. The fortunes of the entire Middle East would change, however, with the discovery of oil. Oil was first found in Persia (Iran), and by 1911 the British-run Anglo-Persian Oil Company (APOC) was successfully exporting Iranian oil. This set off a race to discover additional oil resources in the region, led by the

A farmer plows a field in the traditional way in Oman. Despite increased oil revenues in the country since 1964, traditional agricultural methods predominate. A large percentage of the Omani population are farmers or fishermen, most of them living in rural villages. The most commonly harvested foods in Oman are dates, papaya, coconut, bananas, and a variety of fish.

British company APOC and Standard Oil in the United States. Throughout the 1930s, Western oil companies negotiated with countries along the Persian Gulf for access to their oil resources. Compared to its neighbors, however, Oman was slow to profit from the oil industry. Oman's oil resources were untouched until 1964, when deposits were found near Fahud in the western desert.

While other Arab states profited from the oil business, Oman's economy was poorly managed. Under Sultan Taymur ibn Faysal's leadership, Oman was burdened with an enormous debt. The country owed money to merchants, which the sultan paid by borrowing from the British government in India. The economy of Oman suffered so much under Taymur ibn Faysal's rule that in 1932 he resigned. His son, Sa'id ibn Taymur, took over as sultan of the struggling country. Inheriting a massive debt from his father's reign, he knew that the best way to bring back wealth to Oman was through the sale of oil.

With the British oil industry eager to expand its business and ibn Taymur hoping to revive Oman's economy, the two explored the entire country for its oil resources. To determine what land the oil companies could drill, the sultan had to define his country's borders. The issue of defining Oman's territory brought Sa'id ibn Taymur into conflict with leaders of Saudi Arabia, since the two adjacent countries had not defined their shared border. The main problem was that both sides claimed the Buraimi Oasis as their own.

By 1952, Sa'id ibn Taymur and the imam were able to unite and drive Saudi Arabia out of the Buraimi Oasis. This rare truce between the two Omani leaders was short-lived, however. By 1954, Sa'id ibn Taymur had sold the rights to the oil in Oman's interior. When the exploration teams began searching for oil, the newly elected imam, Ghalib bin Ali, accused the sultan of violating the Treaty of Seeb. This was the 1920 agreement that gave Oman's reigning imam the power to control its interior lands. The conflict that the treaty was

Sa'id ibn Taymur (1910–1972) took the position of sultan in Oman in 1932 after his father's resignation. Despite the discovery of oil in the region during his reign, Oman remained impoverished and isolated. As a conservative Muslim, Sa'id ibn Taymur sought to limit modernization in Oman and enforced antiquated laws, public executions, and slavery of people of African descent. Because of his conservative views, Sa'id ibn Taymur was ousted in a coup on July 23, 1970, and succeeded by his only son and heir, Qabus ibn Sa'id.

written to end had begun again. The imam's brother, Talib, formed an alliance with Saudi Arabia, which still claimed the Buraimi Oasis, against the sultan. He created the Oman Liberation Organization (OLO), intending to drive out the British and make the inland region a separate independent state.

With the help of the British military, the sultan responded to the rebellion by taking control of Ibri, an interior town west of Masqat. Ghalib bin Ali went to the newly formed Arab League to ask it to recognize their independence. The league supported him, mostly because its members opposed the presence of the British in the region, but it was no help. In 1957, the sultan took over Nizwa and al-Rustaq, the imam's capital cities. The sultan soon had control of the entire inland region. With the rebels defeated, the sultan opened the way for oil exploration in Oman by revoking the Treaty of Seeb. Imam

As various tribes tried to isolate Oman's interior from its coast, hoping to protect this territory from development, Sultan Sa'id ibn Taymur wanted to unite the country. He hoped to eliminate Oman's debt by exploiting Oman's petroleum reserves. When the interior tribes rebelled and sought their independence after the death of their religious leader in 1954, the sultan sought military protection from the British. Because the British were also interested in gaining wealth from Oman's petroleum reserves, they were eager to intervene. The British captured Fort Nizwa in 1957, when this photograph was taken.

Ghalib bin Ali was exiled to his home village. His brother, Talib, escaped to Cairo, Egypt. Eighteen months later, Talib returned to make another attack against the sultan. His rebellion was defeated in three months.

Rebellion in Dhofar

In 1958, Sultan Sa'id ibn Taymur moved the capital of Oman to Salalah, which lies in the southern province of Dhofar. He rarely left his palace or met with any of the tribal leaders. The sultan used his power to keep Oman isolated from the changes in ideas and technology that were taking place around the world. Aside from his close relationship with the British government, he had no interest in foreign ideas and cultures. To be permitted to leave the country, an Omani had to get permission from the sultan himself. He was largely opposed to education and political reform. In his view, even items such as eyeglasses or radios were too Western to allow in Oman. The world was rapidly changing, but Sa'id ibn Taymur made sure that Oman would remain sheltered from new ideas, technology, or any other modernization.

Sa'id ibn Taymur had two daughters and one son, Qabus ibn Sa'id. The sultan wanted to keep his son from leaving the royal palace, but his British advisers persuaded him to let Qabus ibn Sa'id study in England. In 1958, Qabus ibn Sa'id left Oman to enroll in a small private school. He studied there for two years and learned to speak English. He entered the Royal Military Academy in 1960, and after completing another two years of study, he was placed with a group of British soldiers in West Germany. While his father chose to remain in his palace, isolated from the rest of the world, Qabus ibn Sa'id traveled to foreign countries and studied other cultures.

People living in Oman began to oppose the isolation that was being imposed on them by Sa'id ibn Taymur. The sultan spent little of the money he collected from the oil industry, leaving his country impoverished. At the same time, a growing number of Omanis believed the sultan was giving up too much of his power to the British government and Western oil companies. This nationalistic spirit reflected an increasingly popular effort to end the influence of Western companies and governments in the Middle East.

In 1965, the United Nations condemned Great Britain for taking too much control over Oman and its neighboring countries, though the organization's efforts to persuade Great Britain to withdraw were unsuccessful.

Armed members of the Yemeni National Liberation Front, who forced the British to withdraw from Yemen, are shown here in 1967. The federation became independent as the People's Democratic Republic of Yemen. Omani soldiers sought inspiration from the members of the Yemeni National Liberation Front in the hopes that their own uprising against the sultan would prove successful.

That same year, ibn Taymur was challenged by a group of rebels from Dhofar that named itself the Popular Front for the Liberation of the Occupied Arabian Gulf (PFLOAG). PFLOAG intended to overthrow the sultan, cut off the country's ties to the British, and make Oman a Communist country like its neighbor, the People's Democratic Republic of Yemen (PDRY). Yemen gave money and weapons to support this rebellion, as did other Communist countries such as China and the Soviet Union. A group of soldiers from Dhofar came close to assassinating Sa'id ibn Taymur in 1966. The sultan managed to stay in power until 1970, when a coup would change the leadership of the country.

6 QABUS IBN SA'ID

When Qabus ibn Sa'id returned to Oman from his travels around the world, his father immediately put him under house arrest. Sa'id ibn Taymur feared that his son might try to make Oman more modern. In the time Qabus ibn Sa'id was away, Sa'id ibn Taymur's conservative policies had become unpopular. Both Oman's citizens and its British allies were frustrated that Sa'id ibn Taymur did not spend enough of the profits he collected from the oil industry on improving the nation's infrastructure. Oman remained isolated from the rest of the world.

From Father to Son

On July 23, 1970, civilians and members of the military led a coup, or forced overthrow of the government, that replaced Sultan Sa'id ibn Taymur with his son, Qabus ibn Sa'id. The British, who were also critical of the sultan, aided the coup. Sa'id ibn Taymur fled to London, where he lived in exile until his death in 1972. Qabus ibn Sa'id, now sultan of Oman, replaced his father at the age of thirty.

The rebellion in Dhofar was still active when Sultan Qabus ibn Sa'id came to power. He tried to end it by rebuilding Dhofar's weak economy, which he believed was the source of the unrest. Nearly 25 percent of Oman's development budget went to improving

Qabus ibn Sa'id became sultan after he replaced his father, Sa'id ibn Taymur, in a 1970 coup. Qabus ibn Sa'id suppressed the rebellion of tribes in Dhofar, built transportation and telecommunication systems, and expanded Oman's government administration.

The entire Arabian Peninsula is seen on this U.S. map of the region, produced by the United States's Central Intelligence Agency (CIA). Petroleum reserves are abundant in the Middle East, with the majority of resources located in Saudi Arabia and Iraq. Reserves in Oman are estimated to be about 4.6 billion barrels and are located primarily in the northern region of the country.

homes, schools, and transportation in Dhofar. The sultan also strengthened his military for attacks against the rebels. Several countries helped Qabus ibn Sa'id fight the PFLOAG, which in 1974 shortened its name to the Popular Front for the Liberation of Oman (PFLO). The British air force aided the sultan's attacks, along with several hundred British troops. Oman's military also received support from the Jordanian government and the shah of Iran. The shah, who was fighting the Communist Party in his own country, sent 3,000 ground forces to Oman. There were also countries that supported Oman with money instead of troops, including Abu Dhabi, which gave $200 million, and Saudi Arabia, which set aside its differences with Oman and gave the country $2.5 billion. By 1975, the rebels controlled only 20 square miles (52 sq km) of land. Even though they were no longer a serious threat, the last few rebel groups did not surrender until 1982 when Oman renewed its relationship with Yemen. At that point, Yemen stopped assisting the rebels, bringing an end to the PFLO.

Modernization

Qabus ibn Sa'id took control of Oman at a time when it faced enormous problems, including widespread disease, poverty, and illiteracy. His response was to reverse the way that his father ruled

The Central Bank of Oman (CBO) was established in 1975 and has since helped regulate and promote business in the country. Several specialized banks operating under the wing of the CBO are the Oman Development Bank and the Oman Housing Bank, which both opened in 1977, and the Oman Bank for Agriculture and Fisheries, which opened in 1981.

The Omani men in this photograph are wearing traditional attire consisting of a simple ankle-length gown with long sleeves called a *dishdasha*. Other common accessories for men include a necklace tassel called a *furakha*, which is sometimes dipped in perfume, and the Omani dagger known as the *khanjar*. The khanjar is worn as a symbol of a man's courage and of Oman's history as a tribal society.

the country and make it into a more modern state. In his first speech to the country after the 1970 coup, he announced that he would remove the regulations on travel and imports that had burdened Oman's citizens while his father was in power. He was also eager to spend government money on improving Oman's infrastructure, unlike his father. When oil producers raised their prices in 1973, all nations along the Persian Gulf largely increased their profits from oil sales. Qabus ibn Sa'id used this money to construct modern buildings in Oman's cities and to improve its hospitals and schools. Since 1970, the number of primary schools in Oman has gone from 3 to more than 300.

Qabus ibn Sa'id's efforts to modernize Oman also included changing the structure of the country's government. He did not give up any of his power as sultan, but he did reform the system to allow smaller regions of

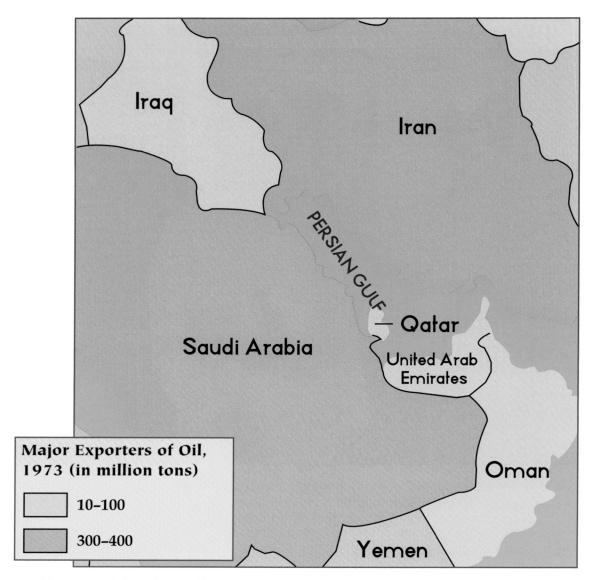

Major Exporters of Oil,
1973 (in million tons)

10–100

300–400

Unlike some of the other Gulf States, such as Iran, that discovered petroleum as early as the 1930s, Oman did not locate similar resources until 1964. As they were positioned in 1973, Saudi Arabia and Iran remain the largest suppliers of oil reserves in the world. In 2002, the combined Gulf States exported about 10.6 million barrels of oil per day, or 27 percent of the world's total imports, according to statistics provided by the U.S. Energy Information Administration. Today, the Gulf States contain about 36 percent of the world's total petroleum supply.

Oman a voice in the government. In the new system, the people living in local inland districts elect a leader who is then approved by the governor of Dhofar. Once approved, the local leaders, or *walis*, represent their districts, or *wilayats*. The result of this arrangement is that the tribal leaders continue to have some authority, particularly in the inland region, though it is to a lesser degree. People living in coastal regions are represented by local deputy governors who do not have to be approved by the governor of Dhofar. In 1981, Qabus ibn Sa'id created the State Consultative

Qabus ibn Sa'id is seen in this 1997 photograph at the head of Oman's national Council of Ministers. The twenty-seven-member council includes a prime minister and three deputy prime ministers overseeing three departments: Security and Defense, Legal Affairs, and Financial and Economic Affairs.

Council (SCC), a fifty-five-member group of walis who represent local interests in the national government. The walis advise the sultan on national affairs. Unlike a parliamentary system, however, the SCC has no real power. It exists only to give advice.

Whether they were elected as walis to represent their district, all of the local tribal leaders, or sheikhs, regularly received money from the national government. As a result, Qabus ibn Sa'id managed to keep the sheikhs loyal. Over the years since this policy was formed, the power of the sheikhs has declined since profits from the oil industry went directly to the national government rather than to tribal leaders.

7 MODERN OMAN

Sultan Qabus ibn Sa'id's efforts to make Oman into a modern state have expanded its economy and given his country a new role in world affairs. When ibn Sa'id took power in 1970, Britain, India, and the United States were the only countries with which Oman had relations. Since that time, ibn Sa'id has dramatically expanded his country's involvement in foreign affairs. Oman became a member of the United Nations in 1971 and has developed closer relationships with countries throughout the West, particularly the United States.

The United States Embassy in Oman opened in 1972. It shared an ambassador with Kuwait until 1974, when a new ambassador to Oman was appointed. The two countries formed a closer relationship in response to the Soviet Union's 1979 invasion of Afghanistan. In an effort to strengthen its military presence in the Middle East, the United States signed a treaty with Oman in 1980 that offered to improve Oman's air and naval bases in exchange for

BAHRAIN

QATAR

SAUDI ARABIA

YEMEN

This is a contemporary map of Oman. Since the 1970s, Oman has made tremendous improvements in its infrastructure, internal relationships with tribal peoples, and economic outlook. Border agreements with the United Arab Emirates were also formalized in 2002. Oman can look forward to a positive future since the rise in the world's oil prices is providing the nation with plenty of revenue and since Oman is discovering new ways to utilize its natural gas reserves.

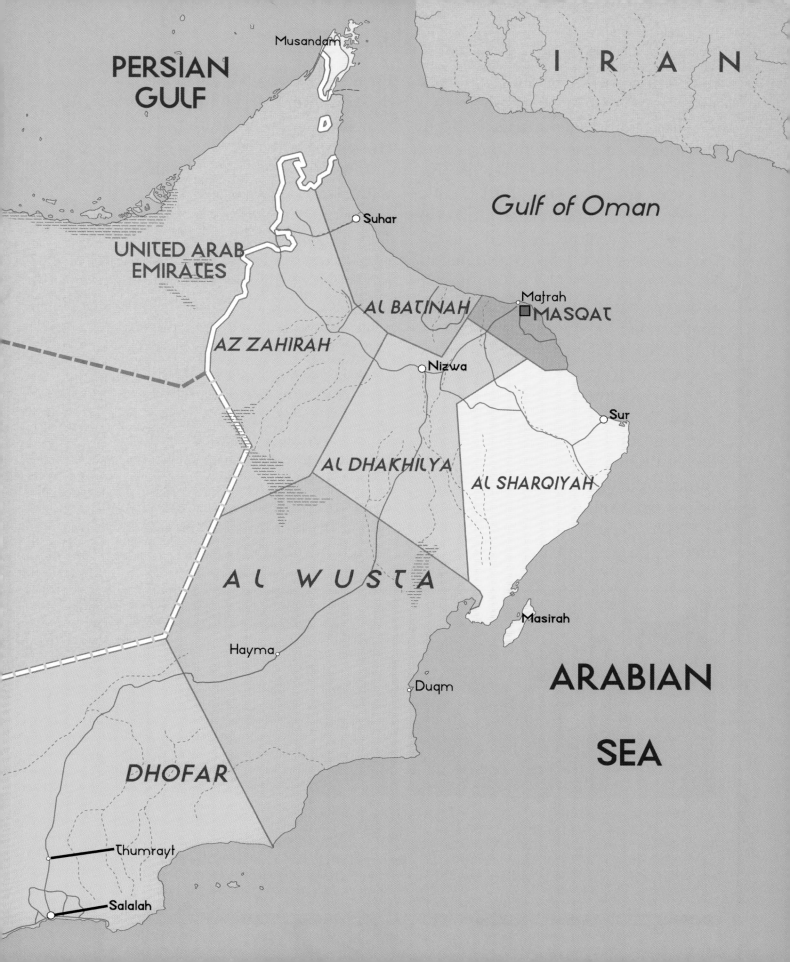

permitting the U.S. military to use them in the case of an emergency.

The United States and its allies put these bases to use several times over the following decades. They became a vital resource for the United Nations during the Persian Gulf War in 1991. When Iraq invaded Kuwait in August 1990, Oman contributed its troops and military bases to the group of more than thirty countries that banded together to drive out the Iraqi army. When the U.S. military responded to the terrorist attacks of 2001 against the United States by pursuing terrorists in Afghanistan, many ground raids that intended to defeat Osama bin Laden's Al Qaeda camps and the Taliban government began from military bases in Oman. In 2003, Oman permitted the U.S. military to use its bases again when President George W. Bush sought to disarm Iraq by leading a military attack against its leader, Saddam Hussein.

Oman's diplomatic relationship with Israel has set it apart from many other countries in the region. The formation of Israel in 1948 sparked bitter opposition throughout much of the Arab world. Oman, however, has maintained warmer relations with Israel than most of its neighbors. Oman was one of only three nations in the Arab League that did not break relations with Egypt after it signed a peace treaty with Israel in 1979. Qabus ibn Sa'id became the first leader of a country in the Persian Gulf region to welcome a representative of Israel when Israeli prime minister Yitzhak Rabin visited him in 1993.

Left: Israeli prime minister Shimon Peres (right), admired a horse belonging to Sultan Qabus ibn Sa'id while on a visit to the Omani resort of Salalah in 1996, his first visit to the Arabian Peninsula. Right: Sultan Qabus ibn Sa'id met with Palestinian leader Yasser Arafat at the Baraka Palace in Muscat, Oman, in January 2002. Arafat briefed ibn Sa'id on the tense situation in the Palestinian territories and American efforts to work toward peace in the region. Oman was one of the few Middle Eastern nations that had worked toward a diplomatic relationship with Israel, but it severed this relationship following the outbreak of Israeli-Palestinian violence in 2000 that killed 360 people.

Modern Economy

Oman's modernization has been so successful that in 1995 the World Bank removed Oman from its list of underdeveloped nations. This is largely the result of the revenue that Oman earns from its oil and natural gas exports. These sales bring in about 90 percent of the government's money.

In 1992, Oman's oil reserves were estimated to be 4.6 billion barrels. Its largest oil fields in Dhofar lie southwest of Masqat. Once the oil has been drilled, pipelines transport it to Mina al Fahal, a port town on the Gulf of Oman. Once there, it is loaded onto ships and exported around the world. The biggest buyers of Omani oil are Japan and Singapore. Oman's vast reserve of natural gas is estimated to fill 17 trillion cubic feet (481 million cubic meters). Most of Oman's energy is fueled by natural gas.

Although oil is the country's most profitable export, the amount that Oman produces is small compared to its oil-producing neighbors. Agriculture is still a vital part of Oman's economy, and it employs 58 percent of its working populace.

One of the most commonly grown crops is the date palm, which can be spotted throughout Oman. The sticky sweet dates are harvested and eaten fresh from June to September. Oman is also a major producer of limes, which grow year-round. Other important cash crops include bananas and melons.

The newest and fastest growing industry in Oman's economy is tourism. Not long ago, it was difficult for tourists, even from neighboring countries, to obtain permission to visit Oman. Having dropped most of these barriers in recent years, Oman's government has drawn the interest of tourists by making extensive restorations of its ancient forts and mosques. In 1995, about 50,000 people traveled to Oman. This number continues to grow as more and more visitors experience its historic sites, artistic treasures, and cultural traditions.

Even with its somewhat dwindling oil resources, Oman may look forward to a bright future, fueled by a growing industrial economy, a strong sense of nationalism and history, and diplomatic leaders eager to be a part of a peaceful Middle East.

TIMELINE

3000 BC A region called Magan flourishes on land that is now part of Oman.

563 BC The Persian Empire conquers northern Oman.

AD 100 Tribes from southern Arabia begin to migrate into Oman.

610 Muhammad spreads the teachings of Islam to Oman.

746 The Omani Ibadites drive the Umayyad rulers out of Oman.

748 Oman's armies conquer Medina.

757 The first Omani imam, Julanda bin Mas'ud, is elected.

1154 A dynasty of kings begins ruling Oman from the island of Hormuz.

1488 Vasco da Gama navigates around the Cape of Good Hope.

1507 Portugal captures Masqat and port towns along the coast of Oman.

1622 The British take control of the island of Hormuz.

1624 Nasir bin Muhammad is elected imam.

1646 Imam Nasir bin Muhammad signs a treaty with the British.

1649 Sultan bin Saif defeats the Portuguese military, ending colonization.

1719 Sultan Saif II dies without an heir, sending Oman into a civil war.

1743 Nadir Shah launches an attack on Oman, capturing Masqat.

1744 Ahmad ibn Sa'id is elected imam.

1748 Ibn Sa'id leads Oman to victory against the Persian military.

1798 Sa'id bin Sultan signs a treaty establishing British protection of Oman.

1809 Bin Sultan launches an attack against Wahhabi tribes.

1822 Sa'id bin Sultan forbids the sale of slaves to Christian nations.

1833 Oman signs a Treaty of Friendship with the United States.

1856 Sa'id bin Sultan dies and his territory is divided.

1862 Zanzibar declares its independence.

1882 Oman signs the Exclusive Agreement with Britain.

1895 Rebels loyal to the imam attack the sultan in Masqat.

1920 The interior and coastal regions of Oman sign the Treaty of Seeb.

1932 Sultan Taymur ibn Faysal resigns.

1952 Sultan Sa'id ibn Taymur unites with the imam in a conflict with Saudis.

1954 Sultan Sa'id ibn Taymur sells the rights to Oman's interior oil.

1957 With British aid, the sultan takes over the cities of Nizwa and al-Rustaq.

1958 Sultan Sa'id ibn Taymur moves the capital of Oman to Salalah; Sa'id ibn Taymur's son, Qabus ibn Sa'id, leaves Oman to study overseas.

1964 Oil is discovered in Oman's western desert.

1966 A group of rebels try to assassinate Sultan Sa'id ibn Taymur.

1970 Sa'id ibn Taymur is overthrown in a coup and is replaced by his son.

1971 Oman becomes a member of the United Nations.

1972 The United States Embassy opens in Oman.

1981 Qabus ibn Sa'id establishes the State Consultative Council.

1982 Oman renews relations with Yemen, ending rebellion in Dhofar.

1991 Oman contributes to the UN effort to drive Iraq out of Kuwait.

1993 Prime Minister Yitzhak Rabin visits Sultan Qabus ibn Sa'id in Oman.

2001 Oman allows the United States to use its bases to quell terrorism.

2003 United States uses Oman's bases during its war to disarm Iraq.

GLOSSARY

aflaj An irrigation system that draws underground water to the surface through tunnels.

Al Qaeda A network of Islamic terrorist groups led by Osama bin Laden.

ambassador A person appointed to represent his or her government in another country.

Arab League A group of twenty-one Arab countries in the Middle East and Africa that was founded in 1945 to improve relations among its member nations.

British East India Company Formed in the 1600s, a group of British merchants that received special rights to trade with countries in the Far East, especially India.

caliph A spiritual leader of Muslims. Caliphs led the spread of Islam following the prophet Muhammad's death.

colonization The process in which a country takes control over a foreign land, often by overpowering its government.

Communism A political and economic system based on Marxism in which all property is shared.

coup (coup d'état) French term meaning "blow to the state," referring to an unexpected overthrow of a government by outsiders.

dynasty A series of leaders who are members of the same family.

empire A group of countries that have a single government.

frankincense A fragrant tree gum that is an important part of several ancient religious rituals.

hajj An annual pilgrimage of Muslims to the holy city of Mecca.

Ibadite Islam An Islamic sect founded in ancient Iraq that is led by elected imams.

ice age A period of history when Earth was covered in glaciers.

imam A type of Muslim spiritual leader.

Islam A religion founded by the prophet Muhammad whose followers worship a single god, Allah, and follow the teachings of the Koran.

Koran The sacred book of Islam.

parliament A branch of government in which power is shared by representatives of local districts.

pasha A military or civil officer of Turkey or various countries in Africa, such as Egypt.

sayyid A title for political rulers of Oman.

semite A member of an ancient group of people, such as Hebrews, Phoenicians, and Assyrians, who spoke a Semitic language.

sultan The single political ruler of an Islamic country.

Taliban An armed political group that came to power in Afghanistan in 1994.

wadi A political deputy appointed by an imam.

Wahhabi Islam An Islamic sect founded by Muhammad ibn 'Abd al-Wahhab that is opposed to practices that it believes violate the Koran's central idea that there is only one god.

walis Leaders who represent Oman's local districts in the State Consultative Council.

wilayats Local districts in Oman that are represented by walis.

World Bank An international bank founded to aid governments of economically depressed countries.

FOR MORE INFORMATION

The Sultanate of Oman
2535 Belmont Road, NW
Washington, DC 20008
(202) 387-1980

Web Sites

Due to the changing nature of Internet
links, the Rosen Publishing Group,

Inc., has developed an online list of
Web sites related to the subject of this
book. This site is updated regularly.
Please use this link to access the list:

http://www.rosenlinks.com/
liha/oman

FOR FURTHER READING

Allen, Calvin H. *Oman* (Creation of
the Modern Middle East).
Broomall, PA: Chelsea House
Publishers, 2002.

Barnett, Tracy. *Oman* (Modern Middle
East Nations and Their Strategic
Place in the World). Broomall, PA:
Mason Crest Publishers, 2003.

Foster, Lelia Merrel. *Oman*. New York:
Children's Press, 1999.

Metz, Helen Chapin, ed. *Persian Gulf
States: Country Studies*. Lanham,
MD: Bernan Publishers, 1994.

Tilley, A. F. *Oman*. Broomall, PA:
Chelsea House Publishers, 1987.

Vaughn, Caroline, and the
Metropolitan Museum of Art. *The
Gifts of the Magi: Gold, Frankincense,
and Myrrh*. New York: Little,
Brown & Company, 1998.

BIBLIOGRAPHY

ABC News Online. "Frankincense in the
Ruins." Retrieved April 28, 2003
(http://www.abcnews.aol.com/
sections/scitech/frankincense1217/
index.html).

Chernush, Kay. "On the Frankincense
Trail." *Smithsonian*, October 1998,
pp. 16–19.

Hawthorn, Vic. *Arab Gulf States*.
Berkeley, CA: Lonely Planet
Publications, 1993.

Metz, Helen Chapin, ed. *Persian Gulf
States: Country Studies*. Lanham,
MD: Bernan Publishers, 1994.

Skeet, Ian. *Oman Before 1970: The End
of an Era*. London: Faber and
Faber, 1985.

INDEX

About the Author

Michael Isaac is a freelance writer living in New York City.

Acknowledgment

Special thanks to Karin van der Tak for her expert guidance regarding matters pertaining to the Middle East and Asia.

Photo Credits

Cover (foreground), pp. 1 (foreground), 4–5, 56–57 © 2002 Geoatlas; cover (background), pp. 1 (background), 31 © Royalty-Free/Corbis; cover (left), p. 20 © AKG Photos/Robert O'Dea; cover (top right), pp. 15, 26 © David Halford 2003; cover (bottom right), p. 55 © Corbis Sygma; pp. 6, 8, 27, 51 courtesy of the General Libraries, the University of Texas at Austin; pp. 9, 11 © K. M. Westermann/Corbis; pp. 10, 14 © Christine Osborne/Corbis; pp. 12–13, 16–17, 29, 37, 40–41, 54 maps designed by Tahara Hasan; p. 18 © The Art Archive/The British Library/British Library; p. 19, 52 © Dave G. Houser/Corbis; p. 21 © Kevin Schafer/Corbis; p. 22 © Bojan Brecelj/Corbis; pp. 24–25 © The Granger Collection; p. 28 © The Art Archive/Palace of Chihil Soutoun Isfahan/Dagli Orti; p. 30 © Wolfgang Kaehler/Corbis; pp. 32–33 © Historical Picture Archive/Corbis; p. 35 © Michael Maslan Historic Photographs/Corbis; p. 38 © Bettmann/Corbis; p. 43 © Arne Hodalic/Corbis; pp. 45, 46, 48, 50 © Hulton/Archive/Getty Images; p. 53 © Peter Sanders; p. 58 © AP/Wide World Photos.

Designer: Tahara Hasan; **Editor:** Joann Jovinelly;
Photo Researcher: Elizabeth Loving